Livin

nda Wilson

CTCert, CertEd

Emap Healthcare Ltd
Greater London House
Hampstead Road
London NW1 7EJ

Nursing Times Clinical Monographs are authoritative, concise, single subject publications designed to provide a critical review of material that will be of value to practising nurses, midwives and health visitors. Their authors, all experts in their field, are asked to be challenging and thought-provoking and to stimulate reflection on current practice. *Nursing Times* Clinical Monographs do not seek to be exhaustive reviews but up-to-date overviews; their critical and evaluative nature is designed to promote best practice through consideration of current evidence.

Topics for publication are decided by the editorial advisory board, with input from practitioners. Monographs are then commissioned as near as possible to the publication date to ensure that the information they contain is the latest available. All manuscripts are reviewed by a board member and a clinician working in the field covered.

Every three months, 12–15 new monographs will be published. They will cover subjects suggested by practitioners (see bottom of page) and any major new developments in the field of nursing care. Each publication will be on sale for a limited time, after which it will be withdrawn and, if necessary, replaced with an updated version.

Suggestions for future titles are welcome and should be sent to Simon Seljeflot at NT Books, Emap Healthcare, Greater London House, London NW1 7EJ

Living wills

Linda Wilson, MA (medical ethics), RGN, CTCert, CertEd

There has been considerable interest in the idea of advance directives, or living wills, in recent years, and patients and their carers need to understand what their significance is. The lord chancellor (1997) described living wills as 'a health care decision intended to have effect when a patient loses capacity'. The Law Commission (1995) used the term advance statements because it did not wish to suggest that these anticipatory decisions must always in be made in writing. It was keen to stress that, however communicated, the statement will detail the types of treatment a patient would or would not find acceptable in given situations. Where these advance statements are limited to identifying the treatments a patient would not be willing to accept, the term advance refusal is most commonly used

Background

When living wills were introduced to the UK by the Voluntary Euthanasia Society in the early 1980s they were called advanced directives because this concept was readily understood by doctors. The Voluntary Euthanasia Society has now adopted the term 'living will', as this is what the public is most familiar with.

Part of the stimulus for advance directives derives from a fear of overtreatment at the end of life, mistrust in medical technology or lack of confidence that health professionals will recognise when enough is enough (Sommerville, 1996). Advanced directives are both the symptom and an effect of changing practice.

We now have the ability to care for very premature infants and to extend life far beyond what would previously have been thought possible by the use of such means as life support machines, transplants and cardiopulmonary resuscitation. Treatments currently only dreamed of will be the norm in the next millennium.

Osborne (1994) looked at the growth in the field of biotechnology and concluded that this had acted as a catalyst for the increasing concern about the ethics of medicine. It is often assumed that because so many treatment options are available everyone will want every possible treatment. There is a notion in some quarters that death is the enemy and we must seek to defeat it at all costs. It can be difficult to remember that death is not perceived as the worst option by some people.

Tonelli (1996) wrote: 'As medical practice has evolved from an ideal of the beneficent physician, practising with little guidance from the patient, toward the acceptance of a nearly absolute right of patients to control the means and manner of their health care, the very boundaries of personal autonomy have been met and forced back.'

He failed to understand that patients may have a different set of values to those held by health professionals and that this must be respected. Where the views of doctors and patients are in accord, there is no problem. The difficulty occurs when there is a dispute about what is in the patient's best interests and who is best placed to decide this.

Not so long ago it was rare for patients to be fully informed about a diagnosis of cancer or other life-threatening disease. The prevailing view in medicine was that such knowledge

Notes

could be harmful and thus should not be explored with the patient.

Fins (1994) suggested that doctors may be more worried about reimbursement for their services than the rights and wrongs of futile treatment.

When Louis Kutner coined the term 'living will' at a meeting of the Euthanasia Society of America in 1967 (Lush, 1993) he argued that one could draw a comparison between a legal trust over property and a legal trust over one's own body.

What this means is that you could decide, while you are well, what you would want to happen to your body once you were no longer capable of making your wishes known.

It is vital to remember that this will apply only if and when you become unable to communicate. You reserve the right to destroy a living will at any stage and your contemporaneous wishes will always be respected.

Many patients are concerned that they will be treated actively even when such treatment has little or no hope of success. To spare both themselves and their families this ordeal patients may draw up a living will.

The question of 'futile' medical treatment has been addressed by several authors.

Nelson (1994) suggested that 'futility is sometimes presented as a crowbar whose purpose is to wedge a certain type of decision-making away from patients to give to physicians . . . Social conceptions of what is reasonable and what are worthy ends in medicine need to be invoked and developed to supplant individual conceptions.'

Cranford (1994) concurred and suggested that doctors may sometimes feel strongly that continued treatment may provide no meaningful benefit to the patient.

Veatch (1994) took this forward by questioning who was best placed to decide what is 'the medical good of the patient', and suspected that doctors were not able to make futility judgements.

Swig et al (1996) explored the reasons why doctors offered resuscitation to patients whom they considered unlikely to benefit from it, even though their employers had introduced policies that did not make this necessary. Doctors were agreeing with the non-resuscitation policy and yet still resuscitating futile cases.

The issue of patient competence to make decisions about the areas addressed in living wills is frequently alluded to.

Kutner et al (1991), while accepting that competent patients have a right to refuse treatment, suggested that there may be conflict between 'enhancing the patient's well-being (society's interest in beneficence) and respecting the patient as a self- determining individual (the individual's interest in autonomy)'.

The Institute of Medical Ethics Working Party (1993), while recognising that living wills have value, was quick to recognise that they are no substitute for active participation in decision-making. The difficulty is that the living will comes into effect only when such participation has become impossible.

What happens if an individual who has lost the ability to make decisions changes his or her mind? The working party felt confident that doctors who were in doubt would always presume that the patient wanted to stay alive, although this may mean the patient is subjected to treatments he or she would not have agreed to.

Ryan (1996) suggested that a living will was tantamount to a gamble with one's life, suggesting that if a patient's inability to make decisions is possibly reversible he or she might be deprived of a treatment he or she would have wanted.

Luttrell and Sommerville (1996) countered this by suggesting that it was rare for healthy people to consider making treatment choices in advance and cited the work of Danis et al (1994), which showed that, while some patients changed their minds about treatment options, those who had made a living will seemed to stick to their choices.

Luttrell and Sommerville (1996) also drew attention to the fact that in the USA, where there was a large number of people who supported the notion of dying without undue medical intervention, few had actually made a living will.

Notes

Elpern et al (1993) found that clients who had drawn up a living will were older and saw themselves as less well.

Sommerville (1996) suggested that living wills could only be really effective when the community was able to confront its own mortality. Societies that try to defy death and its inevitability are unlikely to see living wills as useful.

Murphy et al (1996) considered the effect of ethnic origin on advance directives and concluded that there was a statistical difference between Mexican Americans, Korean Americans or African Americans compared to European Americans in accepting a living will and the rate of completion. Americans of European descent were much more likely to have drafted living wills.

Bailly and De Poy (1995) identified that the well-being of older adults was linked to their ability to make autonomous decisions and that advance directives could satisfy this by altering the focus from direct action to having the power to have decisions implemented.

Stechmiller et al (1991) looked at health care workers who had made living wills and found that those who had done so were less likely to have a religious affiliation, were very likely to have been involved in the terminal care of a family member and had either more than 20 years' experience with terminally ill patients or less than one year. The significance of the family member related to respondents' frustration at their inability to influence decision-making, which contrasted sharply with their professional role.

The difficulties of the nominated proxy in deciding what the patient would want is a frequent theme. Perry et al (1995), looking at patients with end-stage renal disease, found that the possession of a living will was seen as very valuable by the patient but the family often wanted the doctor to decide on treatment.

Sulmasy et al (1994) researched the issue of proxies and observed the responses of a group of patients and their proxies in relation to several hypothetical situations. They concluded that living wills were less predictive of personal wishes than discussion and non-church-going behaviour.

Hamel and Lysaught (1994) explored the influence of religious beliefs on palliative care choices, most particularly when relatives believe that only God can give and take life. They found that when the care-givers and the patient's family are from different cultural or religious backgrounds this may rob the patient of the ability to control his or her care. Discussion of the problems of reconciling *Halacha* (Jewish law) and living wills can be found in Schostak (1994).

Emmanuel (1996), Ross and West (1995) and Munoz et al (1989) considered the financial implications of non-implementation of living wills. As much as US$109bn a year could be saved by more rigorous promotion of living wills in the USA.

If we treat patients who have made a valid advance refusal, then not only are we guilty of assault but we are also allocating scarce resources to giving treatment that is not wanted.

However, if we follow advance refusals to the letter there can be problems of causing rather than alleviating suffering, as described by Rosner (1994). In a letter to the *Lancet*, he discussed the case of a terminally ill cancer patient who had developed intestinal obstruction.

Relieving treatment had been tried and failed and she was not responding. The doctors felt that a colostomy was indicated, but the patient's daughter produced a living will made some years earlier which refused heroic measures in the terminal stages of her disease and refused permission. She later relented and the operation was performed. The patient died two days later.

Rosner concluded that the patient suffered more because of the delay of a necessary operation and suggested that the living will or its interpretation had actually harmed the patient.

Conversely, Strother (1991) discussed how not following the instructions in a living will increased the suffering of a patient.

Notes

La Puma et al (1991) were concerned that living wills could be used primarily to contain costs and found this totally reprehensible, especially where ill and disadvantaged patients were concerned.

Making a living will can mean that a treatment you might want may be withheld, but Wilson (1996) identified that her sample population had considered this carefully and still preferred to draw up an advance directive.

Most reported that doing so had given them a sense of regaining control. What is important is that the decision is made freely and without duress. This is where the evidence of the witnesses is vital (Andrews, 1997).

So how can we ensure that a living will works to our advantage? The critical ingredient seems to be a full and frank discussion between the patient, the family and the doctor.

Health professionals must accept that patients have the right to take risks and that, while they need to ensure that patients have met all the criteria for informed consent — sufficient information presented in a format they can understand, mental competence, absence of clinical depression and no coercion — they must then accept the wishes of the patient, whether these accord with their view of his or her best interests or not.

Emanuel (1995) identified that there is a major problem in valuing living wills as tools for direct care and highlighted the need for medical education to address this.

Teno et al (1997) concluded that, despite having drafted very specific advance directives, the care given to this client group was inconsistent with the wishes expressed in the document for half the cases studied.

The legal basis of living wills

Living wills evolved in the USA, where the first statute was the California Natural Death Act 1976. At that time, doctors were much less likely to disclose a terminal diagnosis to patients, so that when they did patients usually had a very limited life expectancy. The statute built in a cooling-off period after drawing up a living will, which meant that the instructions could not apply until at least 14 days had elapsed.

From this beginning, a number of other statutes grew, some of which broadened the definition of 'terminal' to include such conditions as permanent unconsciousness, cancer and dementia.

Lush (1993) drew attention to the Indiana Living Wills and Life Prolonging Procedures Act 1989, which identified that not only might people want to refuse treatment, they might also wish to demand it.

There was no federal legislation in the USA until the Patient Self-Determination Act 1990. La Puma et al (1991) described it as follows: 'The act requires hospitals, nursing homes and hospices to advise patients on admission of their right to accept or refuse medical care and to execute an advance directive . . .

'Provider organisations will also be required to document whether patients have advance directives. Compliance with the act is a condition of Medicare and Medicaid reimbursement and is tied into institutional Medicare contracts.'

Although this appeared to give patients information and choice, La Puma et al (1991) were concerned that acutely ill patients could not make considered rational judgements in discussions, much less when written material was presented to them.

There was also the issue of Medicare and Medicaid — benefits paid to elderly people and those on state support. People in receipt of such benefits tended to be less able to assert their wishes. Silva and Sorrell (1984) found that those who read informed consent statements carefully tended to be Caucasian, better educated and younger than those who did not.

There are a number of organisations that supply the paperwork needed to complete a living will, and their details can be found at the end of this monograph. The Patients Association (1996)

Notes

gives this checklist of the minimum requirements:

- Full name;
- Address;
- Name and address of GP;
- Information as to whether advice was sought from health professionals;
- Signature;
- Date;
- Witness signature;
- A clear statement of wishes, either specific or general;
- If applicable, the name, address and telephone number of the person who has been nominated to be consulted about treatment decisions.

A living will is a document, made voluntarily by a competent individual over 18, in which he or she stipulates which treatments he or she would like to receive or reject in a given set of circumstances.

It should be as specific as possible so that it can be clearly seen that the patient refuses or accepts treatments, such as resuscitation, for instance, in the event of a terminal condition, or artificial feeding in a persistent vegetative state. The closer the match to the condition and the more it has been discussed with health care staff and family members (and the proxy), the greater the chances of the patient's wishes being carried out.

Although living wills were initially linked with the euthanasia movement, it is important to recognise that they are a separate issue. Indeed, in his introduction to the green paper *Who Decides?* (Lord Chancellor's Department, 1997) the lord chancellor clarified that 'the government fully supported the view of the House of Lords' Select Committee on Medical Ethics in its report of February 1994 that euthanasia is unacceptable and cannot be sanctioned in any circumstances . . . So let us not be sidetracked in this debate.'

However, Roman Catholic church leaders were concerned that living wills appeared 'to permit non-voluntary euthanasia by the omission of treatment' and envisaged that 'making legally binding even suicidally motivated refusals of medical treatment given in advance of mental incompetence' could result in vulnerable people being the victims of grave injustice (letter in the *Daily Telegraph*, April 1, 1998).

The lord chancellor repeated his assurances that clarifying the law in relation to living wills was not synonymous with a slide towards euthanasia (letter in the *Daily Telegraph*, April 2, 1998).

The British Medical Association first issued guidelines in 1992 about advance statements. These were amended in 1995 and define advance statements as 'a mechanism whereby competent people give instructions about what is to be done if they subsequently lose the capacity to decide or to communicate'.

While recognising that these could apply to any area of a person's life, the most contentious one is that of medical treatment, especially where it relates to end-of-life issues.

Speaking of advance refusals, the BMA guidance (1995) states that 'an unambiguous and informed advance refusal is as valid as a contemporaneous decision. Health professionals are bound to comply when the refusal specifically addresses the situation which has arisen.'

The difficulty is making sure that living wills are specific enough, given that most are written in broad terms. Living wills cannot demand treatment that would not be appropriate or is illegal. They cannot refuse 'basic care', such as washing, the offer of pain relief and the offer of being fed.

What is the law?

In the UK, there is a common misconception that living wills are not legal. While there is no statute currently governing living wills they are recognised in common law, provided certain criteria have been met.

What is meant by common law? Carson and Montgomery (1989) state that it is 'the collection of judges' decisions about the law on subjects where parliament has not yet passed any statutes'.

Notes

What are the criteria for a living will to be valid?

- The person who has drawn up the living will must have been mentally competent, not suffering from any mental distress and over 18 when he or she made the request;
- The person must have been fully informed about the nature and consequence of the living will when he or she made it;
- The person made it clear that the living will should apply to all situations or circumstances that may arise at a later date;
- The person was not pressurised or influenced by anyone else when he or she made the living will;
- The living will has not been changed, either verbally or in writing, since it was drawn up;
- The person is now incapable of making any decision because he or she is unconscious or otherwise unfit.

Kessel and Meran (1998) said that for a living will to be legally binding 'the patient must have anticipated and intended the refusal to apply to the circumstances that subsequently arise'.

Living wills tend to be written in general terms and may require a measure of interpretation by the drafter's nominated proxy.

Legal precedents in the UK for living wills

Case: Re T (Adult: refusal of medical treatment) [1992] 4 ALL ER 649

A young, heavily pregnant woman, referred to as Miss T, was involved in a road traffic accident on July 1. On July 4 she was admitted to hospital with severe chest pains and diagnosed as having pneumonia, which was treated.

On July 5, while in considerable pain, coughing up sputum, on various drugs and having contractions in the first stage of labour, Miss T informed medical staff that she did not want a blood transfusion and signed a form of refusal to consent but did inquire whether an alternative treatment was possible.

Miss T was not a Jehovah's witness but her mother was a fervent supporter of the faith and had visited her daughter shortly before she reached this decision. Miss T's paternal family were opposed to the sect.

Following an emergency Caesarean section and delivery of a stillborn baby on July 6, Miss T's condition deteriorated and she was transferred to intensive care.

She remained critically ill and on July 8 Justice Ward ruled that she could be given a blood transfusion and that this would not be unlawful in the circumstances.

The question here was whether or not Ms T was under the influence of her mother and whether she had been fully informed when she made her decision. Lord Donaldson in his ruling raised the question of whether or not the decision was freely made.

The principle established as a result of the case was that, where an informed and able patient makes a choice which is 'clearly established and applicable in the circumstances', doctors would be bound by it.

Case: Airedale NHS Trust v Bland [1993] 1 ALL ER 821 [1993] 12 BMLR 64 (HL)

Tony Bland, a keen sports fan, went to Hillsborough football ground on April 15, 1989, to watch his team playing in the semi-final of the FA cup. By the end of that day, 95 people were dead. Mr Bland suffered crush injuries and was subsequently diagnosed as being in a persistent vegetative state.

Medical opinion was unanimous in the diagnosis and agreed that there was no hope of improvement or recovery. The case was the first of its kind in the UK and the judges sought to ensure that their ruling did not set a legal precedent.

Lord Bingham stated the principles that both parties agreed on were as follows: 'It is a civil wrong and may be a crime to impose medical treatment on a conscious adult of sound mind without his or her consent' and 'a medical practitioner must comply with clear instructions given by an adult of sound mind as to the treatment given or not

Notes

given in certain circumstances, whether those instructions are rational or irrational.

This principle applies even if, by the time the specific circumstances pertain, the patient is unconscious or no longer of sound mind'.

This statement supports living wills because it allows the wishes of a competent adult, clearly stated, to be acted on even if doctors do not deem them to constitute rational choices.

Lords Mustill, Goff and Keith all accepted that a health care provider would be guilty of battery if he or she treated a patient who had given a valid anticipatory refusal.

Case: Re C [1994] 1 ALL ER819

In the BMA's report *The Older Person: Consent and Care* (1995), the case of Re C is described as follows: 'A man in his sixties who was confined to Broadmoor Hospital suffered from the delusion that he was medically qualified. C refused amputation of a gangrenous foot and his anticipatory decision to continue to reject such an operation in future was upheld at law.

'Lord Justice Thorpe granted an injunction restraining clinicians from removing the leg at any time — even at a time when C might not be capable of withholding his consent.'

The key feature here is that the client must be clear about the consequences of the decision he or she is taking. The law was not saying that C was capable of making all decisions, but that he could make *this* decision.

Although living wills are a relatively new innovation, we have seen advance refusals before.

The BMA (1995) stated that 'a clear and informed statement refusing blood by a Jehovah's witness is an example of a potentially legally binding document'.

It is worth restating that a living will is a voluntary undertaking and that a competent individual can say at any time that he or she does not want it to apply any longer. Ideally a living will should be reviewed regularly by the individual who has drafted it to ensure that it is still relevant.

What happens to people who have not made a living will?

If an individual is not capable of making treatment choices and has not made his or her wishes known in advance, there are two ways in which doctors can proceed.

The first is by using the concept of 'best interests'.

Beauchamp and Childress (1994) explained this as follows: 'The best interests standard protects another's well-being by assessing risks and benefits of various treatments and alternatives to treatment, by considering pain and suffering, and by evaluating restoration or loss of functioning.'

In the UK, the best interests standard is the one used in health care and in other fields.

In the USA, the more commonly used standard is that of 'substituted judgement'. The essence of this is that the right to make decisions is the patient's alone — being incapable of doing so does not invalidate this right.

Where patients are clearly unable to decide anything, another decision-maker must accept the responsibility of making the decision for them.

The ethical issues surrounding living wills

Living wills come into force when an individual is incapable of making decisions or can no longer make his or her wishes known.

Beauchamp and Childress (1994) named autonomy as a key issue. The principle of autonomy is variously described as mastery of self, the ability to decide for oneself, balancing competing views and deciding on the most appropriate course of action to take. It also involves accepting ownership of decisions that one has made, whether they are subsequently found to be sound or an error of judgement.

Lush (1993) stated that the underlying philosophy of a living will was neither the right to die nor the right to live but the right to choose for oneself. This freedom of choice is generally known in the medical profession as

Notes

autonomy and in the legal profession as the right of self-determination.

Running alongside the notion of personal autonomy is the notion of respecting the autonomy of others. While autonomy is vitally important, we are also charged to act beneficently towards those who are incapacitated. This means to act in that person's best interests. How can we do this and respect a living will?

The Society for the Protection of Unborn Children (SPUC, 1998) states that 'health care professionals always have a duty to act in accordance with the patient's best interests, integral to which are preserving life, restoring health and minimising suffering. Only if tube-feeding is ineffective in providing nourishment or unduly burdensome is its withdrawal in accordance with the person's best interests.'

In this kind of dilemma nurses and doctors can feel torn between saving a patient and respecting his of her decision to refuse to receive a treatment he or she specified in advance. We may feel that we have a much better understanding of the likely outcomes than the patient can reasonably be expected to have.

We have a duty to ensure that we explain the issues clearly but must then accept the right of the patient to disagree with what we propose. Otherwise we are guilty of paternalism — the notion that doctor or nurse knows best.

Autonomous patients have the right to refuse treatment and, as in the case of C described earlier, patients incapable of making rational decisions may be judged by the courts to have this right in relation to specific decisions.

We need to remind ourselves that a living will comes into effect only when the individual is no longer capable of making his or her wishes known.

Kuczewski (1994) asked whether the interests of the competent person who made a living will and those of the incapacitated person he or she has become are sufficiently similar to allow the living will to be applied.

Dresser and Robertson (1986, 1991) posed the question: 'By what right can we apply the judgements encoded in a living will by a competent person at one time to an incompetent person at a later time?'

A living will is necessarily based on what our current interests are. We may thus have to base treatment decisions on the interests of the competent person in the past rather than on the current interests of the person before us.

Buchanan and Brock (1989) suggested that the person who is no longer able to make a decision may still be able to experience some pleasure in his or her damaged existence. Although the pleasure may not be one that the person could have envisaged, can we in good faith enact the living will made when he or she was competent?

And what about the issue of killing and letting die? Whereas the withdrawal of certain drugs that no longer have any therapeutic benefit to the patient is regarded as reasonable by all sides in the debate and should not be confused with passive euthanasia, much concern has been expressed by groups such Healthcare Opposed to Euthanasia (HOPE) about withdrawing feeding in 'hopeless' cases.

HOPE stated in its response to the *Who Decides?* document (Lord Chancellor's Department, 1997): 'Recognising that a majority see tube-feeding in cases of persistent vegetative state as futile treatment in someone who is effectively dead already we, however, are convinced that tube-feeding can be an effective part of the basic care all living human beings deserve simply because they are human and living. To withdraw it in cases of PVS is the intentional killing by omission of someone who is not dying in any previously understood sense of that word.'

SPUC also argued that in any legislation on advance statements the withdrawal or withholding of treatment or care with the intent to cause death must be excluded.

When considering the ethics of any given situation, health care professionals are bound to act in a way that promotes the right of individuals to make informed choices about those issues that directly concern them.

Notes

Within the doctor/patient relationship, the competent patient must consent to the proposed treatment. What is at issue here is whether or not the previously held views of patients should be respected in law when competence has been lost. The lord chancellor is currently considering this issue.

SPUC suggests that advance refusals 'should not simply be presumed to survive any supervening incapacity but should have greater force the more closely they can be shown to reflect the patient's continuing wishes' (SPUC, 1998).

The Voluntary Euthanasia Society says the views of the competent person should be respected above all else. People who have cared for a relative with dementia may not be medically qualified but they may be better placed than doctors to state that there are certain treatments they would not want to have, should they succumb to dementia one day.

Much of the writing against legislating for living wills focuses on whether or not suicide is a reasonable choice for an individual to make.

SPUC says that no conduct (including omissions) intended to cause death is in a person's best interest. While some people may support that view, others will not.

Patients do have the right to do things we may not agree with personally. There is a need for health care professionals to see the bigger picture and, having ensured that the patient is in full possession of the facts, allow him or her to make the decision.

SPUC and HOPE argue cogently for the need to protect people who are no longer able to make competent decisions and, where no anticipatory wishes have been expressed, we have a duty to do so.

With a living will there is a theoretical risk that the patient could change his or her mind when he or she becomes incapacitated, but Wilson (1996) found that people who had drafted living wills preferred to make decisions about their future care and to have them enforced even if this risk existed.

How can a living will be of use to nurses?

We need to remember that living wills are voluntary and not readily available, therefore the individual who makes one has usually considered it carefully.

When nurses assess patients on admission to hospital, there is a section on the admission form relating to death and dying, often referred to as the final activity of living.

Nurses can feel uncomfortable discussing this with patients, but if patients possess a living will they are in effect signalling to us that they are comfortable talking about end-of-life issues.

In doing this, nurses can achieve the following:

- Exploring with patients their concerns and worries and correcting any misconceptions;
- Providing more opportunity for patients to fully participate in their care planning;
- Taking up the role of patient advocate and helping patients to avoid futile interventions not acceptable to them;
- Developing trust and an understanding of the patient's wishes;
- Enabling the patient to have a dignified death free of unnecessary intervention;
- Helping to return control to the patient.

Nurses and doctors should not act as witnesses to a living will (Andrews 1997) but should ensure that the patient has access to the material and people necessary to make an informed choice.

Conclusion

Whether or not living wills become binding in statute law will depend on the outcome of the consultation on *Who Decides?* (Lord Chancellor's Department, 1997). Whether they will ever be widely used or not, a knowledge of what they are and how they can help health care professionals is vital to enable us to offer the best care to patients.

Notes

Living wills should be drafted when the patient is free from the pressure of acute illness, pain and discomfort and could be a useful adjunct to ongoing discussion while the patient is able to participate.

Living wills are entirely voluntary and must never take precedence over the current wishes of competent people. They can be destroyed at any time and become active only when an individual is unable to make his or her wishes known. They can provide useful pointers for discussion and guide us when the person becomes incapable of making decisions. **NT**

References

Andrews, J (1997) Living wills. *Practice Nurse*; 14: 4, 250–254.

Bailly, D.J., De Poy, E. (1995) Older people's responses to education about advance directives. *Health and Social Work*; 20: 3, 223–228.

Beauchamp, T., Childress, J. (1994) *Principles of Biomedical Ethics*. Oxford: Oxford University Press.

British Medical Association (1995) *The Older Person. Consent and Care*. London: BMA.

British Medical Association (1995) *Views on Advance Statements*. London: BMA.

Buchanan, A.E., Brock, D.W (1989) *Deciding for Others: The Ethics of Surrogate Decision-Making*. New York: Cambridge University Press.

Carson, D., Montgomery, J. (1989) *Nursing and the Law*. London: Macmillan Press.

Cranford, R.E. (1994) Medical futility: transforming a clinical concept into legal and social policies. *Journal of the American Geriatrics Society*; 42: 894–898.

Danis, M., Garrett, J., Harris, R., Patrick, D.L. (1994) Stability of choices of life-sustaining treatments. *Annals Of Internal Medicine*; 120: 7, 567–573.

Dresser, R. (1986) Death and incompetent patients: conceptual infirmities and hidden values in the law. *Arizona Law Review*; 28: 3, 375–405.

Elpern, E., Yellen, S., Burton, L. (1993) A preliminary investigation of opinions and behaviors regarding advance directives for medical care. *American Journal of Critical Care*; 2: 2, 161–167.

Emanuel, L. (1995) Advance directives: Do they work? *Journal of the American College of Cardiology*; 25: 1, 35–38.

Emanuel, E. (1996) Cost-savings at the end of life: what do the data show? *Journal of the American Medical Association*; 275: 24, 1907–1914.

Fins, J. (1994) Futility in clinical practice. Report on a congress of clinical services. *Journal of the American Geriatrics Society*; 42: 8, 861–865.

Hamel, R., Lysaught, M. (1994) Choosing palliative care: do religious beliefs make a difference? *Journal Of Palliative Care*; 10: 3, 61–66.

Healthcare Opposed to Euthanasia (1998) *Submission to the Lord Chancellor's Department*. London: HOPE.

Institute of Medical Ethics Working Party (1993) Advance directives: partnership and practicalities. *British Journal of General Practice*; 43: 369, 169–171.

Kessel, A., Meran, J. (1998) Advance directives in the UK: legal, ethical and practical considerations for doctors. *British Journal of General Practice*; 48: 430, 1263–1266.

Kutner, J., Ruark, J., Raffin, T. (1991) Defining patient competence for medical decision-making. *Chest*; 100: 5, 1404–1409.

Kuczewski, M. (1994) Whose will is it anyway? A discussion of advance directives, personal identity, and consensus in medical ethics. *Bioethics*; 8: 1, 27–48.

La Puma, J., Orentlichner, D., Moss, R.J. (1991) Advance directives on admission. *Journal of the American Medical Association*; 266: 3, 402–405.

Law Commission (1995) *Report 231*. London: Law Commission.

Lord Chancellor's Department (1997). *Who Decides? Making Decisions on Behalf of Mentally Incapacitated Adults*. London: HMSO.

Lush, D. (1993) Advance directives and living wills. *Journal of the Royal College of Physicians of London*; 27: 3, 274–277.

Luttrell, S., Sommerville, A. (1996) Limiting risks by curtailing rights: a response to Dr Ryan. *Journal of Medical Ethics*; 22: 2, 100–104.

Munoz, E., Chalfin, D., Birnbaum, E. et al (1989) Hospital costs, resource characteristics and the dynamics of death for hospital patients in cardiology diagnosis related groups. *Heart and Lung Journal of Critical Care*; 18: 2, 164–171.

Murphy, S., Palmer, J., Azen, S. et al (1996) Ethnicity and advance care directives. *Journal of Law, Medicine and Ethics*; 24: 2, 108–117.

Nelson, J. (1994) Families and futility. *Journal of the American Geriatrics Society*; 42: 8, 879–882.

Notes

Osborne, T. (1994) Power and persons: on ethical stylisation and person-centred medicine. *Sociology of Health and Illness*; 16: 4, 515–535.

Patients Association (1996) *Advance Statements about Future Medical Treatment*. London: Patients Association.

Perry, D., Molzahn, A., Nicholas, D., Dossetor, J. (1995) Attitudes of dialysis patients and care-givers regarding advance directives. *ANNA Journal*; 22: 5, 457–481.

Robertson, J. (1991) Second thoughts on living wills. *Hastings Benter Report*; 21: 6, 6–9.

Rosner, F. (1994) Living wills (letter). *The Lancet*; 343: 8904, 1041.

Ross, P., West, D. (1995) Advance directives: the price of life. *Nursing Economics*; 13: 6, 355–361.

Ryan, C.J. (1996) Betting your life: an argument against certain advance directives. *Journal of Medical Ethics*; 22: 2, 95–99.

Schostak, R. (1994) Jewish ethical guidelines for resuscitation and artificial nutrition and hydration of the dying elderly. *Journal of Medical Ethics*; 20: 2, 93–100.

Silva, M.C., Sorrell, J.M. (1984) Factors influencing comprehension of information for informed consent: ethical implications for nursing research. *International Journal of Nursing Studies*; 21: 4, 233–240.

Society for the Protection of the Unborn Child (1998) *Beyond Autonomy. Response to the Green Paper Who Decides?* London: SPUC.

Sommerville, A. (1996) Are advance directives really the answer? And what was the question? In: McLean, S.A. (ed) *Death, Dying and the Law*. Aldershot, Hampshire: Dartmouth Publishing.

Stechmiller, J.K., Conlon, M., Anderson, G. (1991) Selected characteristics of nurses and physicians who have made living wills. *Death Studies*; 15: 2, 119–130.

Sulmasy, D.P., Haller, K., Terry, P.B. (1994) More talk, less paper: predicting the accuracy of substituted judgments. *American Journal of Medicine;* 96: 5, 432–438.

Strother, A. (1991) Drawing the line between life and death. *American Journal of Nursing*; 91: 4, 24–25.

Swig, L., Cooke, M., Osmond, D. et al (1996) Physician responses to a hospital policy allowing them not to offer cardiopulmonary resuscitation. *Journal of the American Geriatrics Society*; 44: 10, 1215–1219.

Teno, J., Licks, S., Lynn, J. et al (1997) Do advance directives provide instructions that direct care? *Journal of the American Geriatrics Society*; 45: 4, 508–512.

Tonelli, M. (1996) Pulling the plug on living wills. *Chest*; 110: 3, 816–822.

Veatch, R. (1994) Why physicians cannot determine if care is futile. *Journal of the American Geriatrics Society*; 42: 8, 871–874.

Wilson, L. (1996) *Living Wills: Are they Worth the Paper they are Written on?* (unpublished MA thesis). Keele, Leicestershire: Keele University.

Further information

Healthcare Opposed to Euthanasia
c/o Christian Medical Fellowship
157 Waterloo Road
London SE1 8XN
Tel: 0171-928 4694

Patients Association
PO Box 935
Harrow, Middlesex
HA1 3YJ
Tel: 0181-423 8999

Voluntary Euthanasia Society
13 Prince of Wales Terrace
London W8 5PG
Tel: 0171-937 7770

Notes

Literature search

To ensure that a balanced and extensive literature search was undertaken, the author used the following databases:

- CINAHL — covers a broad range of nursing literature and is available on computer or in book form in most hospital libraries;
- Medline — includes a wide range of medical journals;
- BIDS — University of Bath database; the social sciences section has a variety of ethics journals;
- Electronic Telegraph — a free service on the net with a search facility to the archive.

If you wish to use these databases, try your hospital or university library. Some journals will be held locally. Librarians also have access to NUJL, which is an interlibrary loan managed by the various libraries. Difficulty will arise if you want the more obscure journals where a British Library request is needed, and these will cost you money. Good articles often have comprehensive reference lists. Another hint is to look at some of the articles and see who is commonly referred to. This indicates a significant text that may be worth trying.

Notes

Notes